THE LITTLE BOOK OF TREES

Illustrated by Caroline Attia
Written by Claire Philip

This book was conceived, edited, and designed by Little Gestalten

Edited by Robert Klanten and Friederike Christoph

Fact check: Ludwig Stegink-Hindriks, forester and head of development, nature and ecosystem, at Niedersächsische Landesforsten, Braunschweig, Germany

Design and layout by Melanie Ullrich

Typefaces: *Sofia* by Olivier Gourvat, *Filmotype Austin* by Jim Lambert

Printed by Printer Trento, S. r. L., Trento
Made in Europe

Published by Little Gestalten, Berlin, 2025
ISBN 978-3-96704-771-4

1st printing, 2025

© Die Gestalten Verlag GmbH & Co. KG, Berlin, 2025

All rights reserved. No part of this publication may be reproduced or transmitted in any form or by any means, electronic or mechanical, including photocopy or any storage and retrieval system, without permission in writing from the publisher

Respect copyrights, encourage creativity!

For more information, and to order books, please visit: gestalten.com/collections/little-gestalten

Die Gestalten Verlag GmbH & Co. KG
Mariannenstrasse 9–10
10999 Berlin, Germany
hello@gestalten.com

Bibliographic information published by the Deutsche Nationalbibliothek

The Deutsche Nationalbibliothek lists this publication in the Deutsche Nationalbibliografie; detailed bibliographic data are available online atdnb.de

 This book was printed on paper certified according to the standards of the FSC®

The Little Book of Trees

Caroline Attia
Claire Philip

LITTLE
gestalten

Contents

- 4 **What Is a Tree?**
- 6 **How Do Trees Grow?**
- 8 **A Year in the Life of a Tree**
- 10 **The Life Cycle of a Tree**
- 12 **Leaves, Flowers, Fruits and Cones**
- 14 **Roots, Trunks, Bark, and Branches**
- 16 **Super Seeds**
- 18 **Let's Go to the Forest!**
- 20 **Deciduous Forests**
- 21 **Tropical Rainforests**
- 22 **Coniferous Forests**
- 24 **Deciduous Trees Around the World**
- 28 **Coniferous Trees Around the World**
- 32 **Fruit Trees Around the World**
- 34 **Nut Trees Around the World**
- 36 **Trees and Us**
- 38 **Trees and You**
- 40 **True or False?**
- 41 **Let's Get Crafty!**

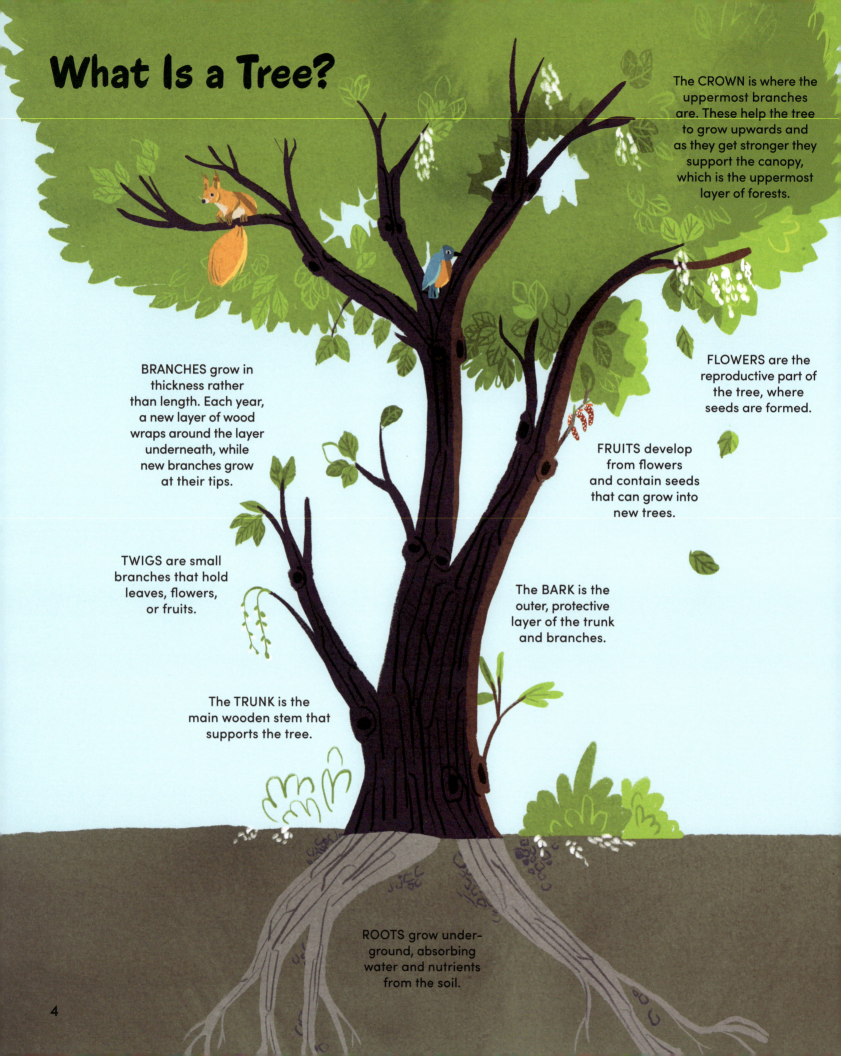

Trees grow all over the world, but have you ever stopped to ask yourself what exactly a tree is?

A tree is a special type of plant with one sturdy stem called a trunk. This trunk, made of wood, supports the tree's branches, leaves, flowers, and fruits. Trees grow their whole life long. They can live for a very long time. A baobab tree, for example, can live for over 1,000 years and mighty oaks can thrive for centuries!

The diversity of trees is amazing. They come in all shapes and sizes: there are more than 70,000 species around the globe, from towering redwoods to delicate cherry trees. The tallest in the world is a coast redwood, which can reach an incredible 380 feet (116 meters) in height—that's 65 feet (20 meters) taller than London's Big Ben clock tower and 75 feet (23 meters) taller than New York's Statue of Liberty!

Trees are important for many reasons. They provide us with oxygen, a gas that is part of the air we breathe, and they help cool the planet by absorbing carbon dioxide, a gas that stores heat in Earth's atmosphere. The Earth's atmosphere is a layer of gases that surrounds the planet.

As well as being essential for life on Earth, trees provide shelter for wildlife such as birds and squirrels and a place to make their homes. Trees also give us fruit and nuts to eat and wood for building and to turn into paper for books. And they are beautiful.

Let's explore the wonderful world of trees!

DID YOU KNOW?
Some trees can communicate! Through their roots, trees can share nutrients (food) with each other and even send warning signals about pests or diseases. This network system shows just how connected with their environment trees really are!

How Do Trees Grow?

Trees need sun, air, water, and nutrients to stay strong and healthy. There is a very special growth layer beneath the bark, which continues to grow in two directions every year. As it grows inwards, it creates a new layer of wood within the roots, trunk, branches, and twigs every year. On the outside (but still under the bark), new cells and pathways develop, which are used to transfer sap (the tree's food) from the leaves to the roots. This makes the tree thicker, especially at the trunk and roots.

From roots to leaves

Water and minerals migrate along the new layer of wood in the trunk and branches from the roots up into the leaves.

Meanwhile the sap that the tree produces in the leaves is in turn transported through the inner layer of bark from the branches via the trunk to the roots. This helps the tree to grow upwards at the crown—at the ends of the branches, where new ones appear during each growth phase.

Making food

With the help of sunlight, leaves turn air and water into a clear, sugary liquid called sap, which is the tree's food. The process by which sap is produced is called photosynthesis, which also produces the gas oxygen. We breathe oxygen in with the air and could not survive without it.

DID YOU KNOW?
The air we breathe is made up mostly of nitrogen, with oxygen making up a smaller part, along with tiny amounts of carbon dioxide and another gas called argon.

Helping the environment

As trees grow, they don't just get bigger—they also help the environment. They provide shelter for all kinds of wildlife, their roots help to anchor the tree within the soil, which prevents soil erosion, and their leafy crowns create shade. By absorbing carbon dioxide, they help to manage Earth's weather systems, and by producing oxygen they support life on Earth—incredible!

A Year in the Life of a Tree

Some trees change with the seasons: in spring, they grow fresh leaves and flowers called blossom. In summer, their branches are full of leaves, fruits, nuts, berries, and seeds. In fall, their leaves drop to the ground, and in winter, the branches are bare. This type of tree is called deciduous. Trees in the tropics often grow all year round. This is because there are only dry seasons and rainy seasons—it is always warm and humid. This is why tropical trees often have no growth rings.

Spring

Springtime is a season of epic growth. Each year, trees grow more wood around their trunks and branches, making them wider. This forms rings in the trunks, which can only be seen if the tree is cut down. In spring, buds that formed the previous year open up as the weather gets warmer, producing new leaves and flowers.

Summer

In summer, deciduous trees are covered in leaves, ripe fruits, nuts, and seeds that feed wildlife. During this season, they also make and store most of their own food ready for winter using photosynthesis. They take in water from the soil and carbon dioxide from the air. Using sunlight and a green pigment (color) called chlorophyll in their leaves, they make their food and release oxygen.

DID YOU KNOW?
Even in winter, some trees keep their leaves. Evergreen trees, like pine and fir, have special leaves that look like needles. These leaves need less food and water, so they stay green and on the tree all year round (see page 22).

Fall

In fall the days become shorter, so there is less sunlight. This means that trees make less chlorophyll, so their green leaves turn orange, yellow, and red. Eventually the leaves fall to the ground, creating a crunchy carpet. These fallen leaves will decompose (break down) and help form a new layer of soil.

Winter

In winter, deciduous trees look bare without their leaves but they are still alive. Most of trees' nutrients are stored in their roots, which continue to grow slowly underground. Some trees still have berries in winter, which hungry birds can feed on. Over the cold months, trees rest quietly, waiting for spring to come again.

The Life Cycle of a Tree

The journey a tiny seed takes to become a mature tree is truly remarkable! Each stage is essential for the development of the tree and the whole cycle can take many years. Even when a tree dies, it still has an important role to play for the wildlife in its environment: dead trees provide shelter, food, and nutrients for birds, insects, and fungi.

During the first stage of the cycle, the seed sprouts into a small seedling, then it grows into a sapling, eventually maturing into a strong tree able to make seeds of its own. When old trees die nutrients are returned to the soil.

1. Starting as a seed

Every tree begins as a small seed. This contains everything the tree needs to grow. When it has received enough water, sunlight, and nutrients the seed begins to germinate: it opens and a small root starts to grow and push into the soil, anchoring itself and taking in the water and nutrients it needs to get bigger.

8. Decay and renewal

Eventually, the tree may die and fall to the ground. Its wood and roots break down and become part of the soil, enriching it with nutrients. These nutrients help new plants and trees to grow, continuing the cycle of life in the forest!

7. Slowing down

As the tree enters old age, its growth slows down and it may show some signs of damage from weather. It may not produce as many leaves, fruits, or seeds as before but it is still very important, as it continues to provide a home for wildlife. As with the branches and leaves, the growth of the roots slows down.

2. The seedling

First the root of the seedling sinks downwards. Then the shoot and small seedling leaves unfold upwards and stretch towards the sun. The energy for this process comes from the seed's supply of starch.

3. The sapling

The plant continues to grow, forming its first leaves. With their help, food is produced for the tree and oxygen for the air we breathe. The plant is still small, but it already has strong roots that grow deeper and deeper into the earth. The plant is now able to create the energy it needs for its own growth.

4. Gaining strength

Once the tree grows a bit taller and thicker, it becomes a sapling. This stage is marked by lots of growth and the development of more branches and leaves. The roots continue to spread outwards and downwards, forming a strong network to support the tree.

5. Becoming a young tree

As the sapling continues to grow, it develops into a young tree with a crown of leaves and a thicker trunk. The young tree is now more resilient, meaning it can cope with challenging weather, such as strong winds and heavy rain. The roots help the tree stay steady during difficult conditions.

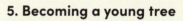

6. Reaching full size

A tree is said to be mature when it has reached its full height and width. This is the stage when it starts to produce seeds, fruits, or nuts, depending on the species. The mature tree is an essential part of its environment and already helping wildlife. By now, the root system reaches well beyond the tree's crown, supporting the tree and storing nutrients and water.

Leaves, Flowers, Fruits and Cones

There are lots of ways to identify a tree. One of the most common is looking at the shape, edges, and arrangement of its leaves. Every tree is slightly different, so this helps us work out what species it belongs to. Have you seen any of these leaves?

Lime

Gingko

Cypress

Pine

Oak

Flowering trees

Many trees grow flowers. Some of these are easy to see, like the pretty pink or white blossoms of cherry trees in springtime, while others are tiny and hard to spot, like those that grow on oak trees. Different kinds of flowering trees bloom at different times of the year.

From blossom to fruit

Did you know that a tree's flowers become its fruit? It's true! For this to happen, the flowers need to be pollinated. Pollination is when insects such as bees collect pollen on their bodies and move it from flower to flower, fertilizing them. Once a flower's petals have fallen off, the part that is left grows into a fruit, which has seeds inside. These seeds can grow into new trees!

Cool cones

Conifer trees such as pine, fir, and spruce grow beautiful from their flowers. Inside the tightly closed cones are the seeds. When the weather is warm enough, the cones open up and the seeds fall out and are scattered around. Some cones only open when they are rotting. Cones come in different shapes and sizes, from small and rounded to long and slender.

DID YOU KNOW?

Birds, insects, and other small animals, such as bats, make their homes in the treetops. They build nests, find food, and raise their young in the safety of the branches. Look up and see.

Roots, Trunks, Bark, and Branches

Let's look more closely at the woody parts of a tree: the roots, trunk, bark, and branches. These parts all work together to keep the tree alive and thriving, and are vital parts of its structure.

Branches

Tree branches grow from the trunk and spread out in different directions. They support the tree's leaves, helping them reach sunlight. Sometimes, when a branch dies or is cut back, the tree continues to grow around the spot where the branch was growing. This leaves a mark on the tree known as a knothole.

Who lives in the branches?

Tree branches make excellent homes for wildlife because they are high off the ground, keeping them safe from predators (animals that hunt other animals to be their food). Birds and squirrels build nests for their young up in the branches, and in some countries larger animals like koalas use them as a resting place.

DID YOU KNOW?

If a tree is cut down, you can see its growth rings. A new ring grows each year, so if you count them you can work out the age of he tree!

Super Seeds

Seeds are the beginnings of new trees! Even the tiny pips inside an apple have the potential to grow into a whole new apple tree. Each seed is unique and they come in a huge variety of shapes, sizes, and colors, depending on the type of tree.

But what came first, the seed or the tree? Have a guess!

Long ago, trees didn't have seeds—plants would use tiny spores to spread and sprout, just like ferns and mosses do today. Spores are like dust that is blown around by the wind, but they are sensitive and need a lot of water to grow. Seeds developed about 360 million years ago: they are much stronger than spores and have a solid shell that protects them, which has helped trees survive better. So that is how trees came to exist before seeds.

DID YOU KNOW?

A seed forms when a tree's flower is pollinated. Inside the seed is a tiny plant and the food it needs to start growing if it lands in soil. Amazing! From the small seeds of a birch tree to the large acorns of an oak, these little packages all carry the potential for new trees.

If a seed lands close to its parent tree, it may struggle to get enough sunlight. However, the older tree can share nutrients with the seedling through its root system, helping it grow.

Maple seeds

Seeds that fall from a tree often land next to their parent tree. The wind, the rain or even animals then carry the seeds further away. Some seeds, like those of the maple tree, are designed to spin through the air like tiny helicopters, while others may be buried by squirrels who sometimes forget where they've hidden them, giving them the chance to sprout into a new tree!

Let's Go to the Forest!

A forest is much more than a collection of trees: it is a wonderful ecosystem where trees, plants, animals, and tiny living things called microorganisms all live and interact with each other. Forests cover around one third of the surface of our planet and are home for most of the world's land animals and plants, providing them with food and clean air. Countries such as Russia, Brazil, and Canada have enormous forested areas.

Lungs of the Earth

There are many types of forest around the world, from dense rainforests to open woodlands. As you explore one, you might come across winding paths that lead you through the trees, clearings where sunlight pours in, or even small streams—all of these have an important role to play in the forest.

Forests are sometimes called the lungs of the Earth because they filter the air and help to keep it clean by absorbing huge amounts of carbon dioxide each year. Forests are also vital for storing water in the soil and act a bit like natural sponges by managing water flow. This reduces flood risks and provides a water supply during dry periods. Unfortunately, harmful human activities like deforestation (the clearing of large areas of trees) and climate change (long-term changes in the Earth's temperature and weather patterns) are affecting forests' survival. Without them natural processes that support life will be disrupted, so we must do more to protect them.

DID YOU KNOW?

Reforestation is the process of replanting trees in areas where forests have been cut down or destroyed. It is an important way to help protect our planet. Another way to protect our forests is to reduce how many trees are cut down for building and farming.

Deciduous Forests

Forests of deciduous trees—trees that lose their leaves each fall, like oaks, maples, beeches, and birches—are found in places that have four seasons, such as parts of North America, Europe, and Asia. Before they fall off, the leaves turn red, orange, and yellow, and once on the ground, they enrich the soil, encouraging other plants to grow. Fungi also thrive on the forest floor, breaking down dead leaves and pushing nutrients back into the soil. When spring comes, new green leaves grow, soaking up sunlight to make food for the trees. Animals that live in these forests include deer, foxes, squirrels, and different kinds of birds.

Tropical Rainforests

These are found near the equator, the imaginary line that runs around the center of the Earth, where it's warm and rainy all year. The Amazon rainforest, in South America, is the largest in the world, covering an area twice the size of India. In tropical rainforests, the trees can grow to be 200 feet (60 meters) tall and together form a thick canopy of leaves, blocking out most of the sunlight. This creates a cool, damp environment below that's perfect for creatures such as ants, poison dart frogs, jaguars, monkeys, anacondas, and toucans. Plants like lianas, orchids, bromeliads, and bamboo also thrive in these conditions.

DID YOU KNOW?

A palm tree looks like a tree, but it isn't one! It has a tall, bendy stem instead of a thick trunk and is part of a plant group that includes grasses.

Coniferous Forests

Coniferous trees are known for their needle-like leaves and cones, which protect their seeds. These trees are well suited to cold environments, like those found in the far north of the world and around mountains. Unlike deciduous trees, coniferous ones keep their needles all year round, which allows them to photosynthesize and make food for themselves even in winter. This means coniferous forests are green and vibrant no matter how cold it gets.

DID YOU KNOW?
The boreal forests cover an area of around 6 million square miles (15 million square kilometers) and make up the largest contiguous (connecting) forest complex on Earth.

Snow forests

Taiga, also known as boreal or snow forest, stretches across parts of North America, Europe, and Asia. These forests are full of coniferous trees like pine, spruce, and fir and have long, harsh winters and short, cool summers. Despite the difficult conditions, they are home to many animals, such as moose, wolves, and bears. In some parts of the taiga, the ground is permanently frozen—this layer is called permafrost.

Coniferous forests are home to some of the most amazing natural wonders on Earth—for example, the bristlecone pine, which can live for close to 5,000 years, making it one of the oldest-living things on the planet. The coastal redwood can grow to be over 300 feet (100 meters) tall and 26 feet (8 meters) wide, making it one of the world's largest trees.

DID YOU KNOW?
Coniferous forests are also very resilient. Some trees, like the lodgepole pine, have cones that only open and release seeds in the high heat of a forest fire!

Needle forests

These forests are commonly found in Europe, particularly in mountainous areas. The needle-like leaves of the trees are adapted for snowy climates as their shape allows snow to slide off easily, which stops branches from snapping. Needle forests are important habitats for wildlife such as deer, foxes, and owls. The Black Forest in Germany, known for its dense, dark woods, is a famous example of a Needle forest.

Deciduous Trees Around the World

Deciduous trees come in all shapes and sizes. Some, like the European alder, have rounded leaves, while others, such as the maple tree, have leaves with sections that stick out—a bit like the fingers on your hand. Their blossoms can be small and delicate or big and colorful. Deciduous trees also produce different types of fruit, like apples and cherries.

Oak

Oak trees produce up to 330 pounds (150 kilograms) of acorns per year. Acorns can grow on their tree for up to 18 months and, when planted in the right conditions, each one can become a mighty oak. Oaks blossom from spring to early summer and have particularly hard wood—the water cities of Venice and Amsterdam are built on oak piles.

Lime

Lime trees can be found in Europe, North America, and parts of Asia. They grow in forests and along roads and reach a height of 98 feet (30 meters). When lime trees blossom, usually in early summer, a sticky layer often forms underneath them: this is caused by aphids, which suck the sap from the leaves and then excrete the sticky liquid.

Elm

Elms grow on riverbanks, in parks, and in cities. They can grow to be up to 115 feet (35 meters) tall. Elm trees have small, flat seeds that are easily carried away and spread by the wind. In the past, wagon wheels would often be made from elm wood because it can be bent but remain very strong.

Chestnut

Chestnut trees grow in forests, on riverbanks, in parks, and in gardens, reaching 66 feet (20 meters) in height. There are two types of chestnut: Sweet chestnuts are edible, while horse chestnuts are poisonous to humans but edible for some animals.

Weeping willow

Weeping willows are so-called because their long branches hang downwards in a shape that resembles a mourning pose. They grow near rivers, lakes, and ponds and are able to survive there because they can fend off the fungi that like to grow in damp environments.

Beech

The beech can grow to be 130 feet (40 meters) tall, producing fruits called beechnuts, which are edible for humans if properly prepared. These trees bear a particularly large amount of fruit every few years—when this happens it is called a mast year.

Birch

You can recognize the birch by its white bark, which can be easily peeled off in strips. Birches grow in temperate and cool climate zones in the northern hemisphere. They blossom in spring and can grow to be 98 feet (30 meters) high.

Baobab

Native to Africa, Madagascar, and Australia, baobabs are commonly found in savannas (an area with widely spaced trees). They can live up to 2,000 years and their trunks sometimes grow to have a diameter of 30 feet (9 meters). In many African cultures, the tree represents wisdom and the coexistence of man and nature.

Coniferous Trees Around the World

Coniferous trees come in many shapes and sizes, just like their deciduous cousins! Some coniferous trees grow tall and straight, while others, like firs and spruces, are cone- or pyramid-shaped. This makes them popular choices for Christmas trees!

The flowers of coniferous trees become cones. They contain the seeds of the tree. These cones can be tiny—like those of the Eastern hemlock, which are less than 1 inch (1–2 centimeters) long—or as large as a football, like the massive cones of the Coulter pine.

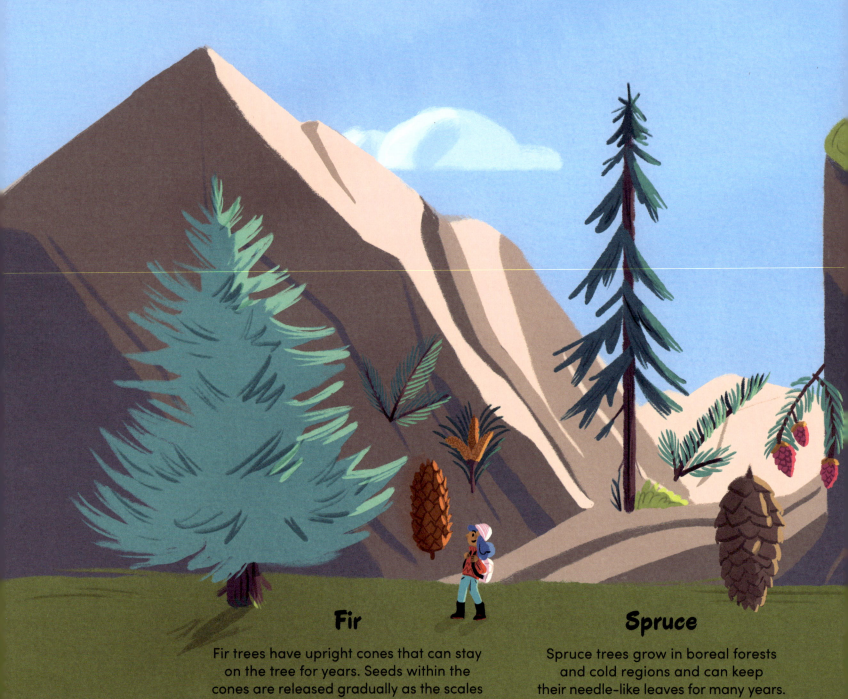

Fir

Fir trees have upright cones that can stay on the tree for years. Seeds within the cones are released gradually as the scales open. Growing in cool, mountainous regions, firs can reach 260 feet (80 meters) and blossom in late spring.

Spruce

Spruce trees grow in boreal forests and cold regions and can keep their needle-like leaves for many years. They flower from late spring to early summer and can be as tall as 200 feet (60 meters).

DID YOU KNOW?
Coniferous Trees usually have needle- or scale-like leaves that help to reduce water loss, which allows them to stay green all year round.

Cypress

Found in warm, temperate areas and subtropical zones, cypress trees flower from late winter to early spring. They grow to an impressive height of 82 feet (25 meters). One of the oldest-living trees in the world is a cypress named Sarv-e Abarkuh, which is growing in central Iran and believed to be more than 4,500 years old.

Pine

Pine trees thrive in a range of climates, from temperate forests and cold, mountainous regions to warm coastal places and even some desert areas! They are true survivors. The oldest pines grow in California, sometimes even at an altitude of 9,840 feet (3,000 meters).

Sequoia

The sequoia grows in the Sierra Nevada, a high mountain range in the west of the USA. It can grow to be over 330 feet (100 meters) tall, blooms in late winter, and has a thick, fibrous bark that protects it from forest fires. Large sequoias grow so thick that it takes a chain of 15 to 20 people to encircle their trunks.

Cedar

The wood of cedar trees is prized for its rich, slightly sweet smell, which comes from its natural oils and has a repellent effect on insects such as moths and fleas. Cedars grow in mountainous regions and in the Mediterranean, reaching a height of up to 115 feet (35 meters), and blooms from late summer to early fall.

Yew

Yew trees often grow in forests and cemeteries and are considered a symbol of immortality. They can grow to be 65 feet (20 meters) high and live up to 1,000 years. Most parts of the tree, such as its needles, bark, and seeds, are poisonous to humans and animals if eaten.

Larch

The larch is found in cooler regions, for example the north of North America and Europe. This conifer can grow to be 150 feet (45 meters) tall. It is different from most other conifers because it sheds its needles in the fall. The wood of the larch is very resistant and robust and is used to build ships and houses.

Fruit Trees Around the World

From the plentiful avocado to the tropical papaya, fruit trees are amazingly diverse. Their leaves can be small and thin, like those of the olive tree, or big and fan-like, as seen on the banana tree. The flowers of fruit trees also vary greatly, from the sweet-smelling blossoms of the orange tree to the soft pink petals of plum trees. And the fruits are wonderfully different too—from the spiky, strong-smelling durian to the sweet mango and the colorful passionfruit.

Cherry

The cherry tree prefers temperate regions with well-drained soil and reaches a height of 26 feet (8 meters). Flowering from early to mid-spring, the pretty blossoms usually only last for one to two weeks and can be easily knocked off by rainfall.

Apple

There are more than 7500 apple varieties in the world, with funny names such as "Pink Lady" or "Granny Smith". They often grow in orchards and gardens and the apple tree blossoms in spring.

Avocado

The Mayans, who lived about 4,000 years ago in what is now Central America, were among the first people to grow avocado trees, which thrive in tropical climates. Did you know that avocados are actually berries with a single, particularly large stone (seed)?

Olive

Hardy and beautiful, olive trees can survive in difficult conditions, such as poor soil and drought. They grow in the Mediterranean, where the summers are hot and dry and the winters are mild and damp. Olive trees blossom from spring to early summer and often live for more than 3,000 years.

Nut Trees Around the World

Trees that produce nuts are known as nut trees. A nut is a type of fruit with a hard shell that protects a single seed inside. Unlike with other fruits, the shell of a nut doesn't open on its own. Instead, it's up to animals, weather, or even fire to disperse the seed.

Nut trees can be found all around the world and include familiar varieties like hazelnut and walnut trees, as well as more unusual ones like macadamia and Brazil nut. Hazelnuts thrive in temperate forests, while Brazil nuts grow in rainforests.

Hazelnut

Strictly speaking there's no such thing as a hazelnut tree: they are bushes, with some of them growing as big as trees and even developing a real trunk, which is why many people mistake them for trees. They are pollinated by the wind rather than insects, and their nuts are a popular ingredient in nougat and chocolate bars.

Pecan

Pecan trees grow in warm regions of North America. They are often found on the banks of rivers and streams and grow to be 130 feet (40 meters) tall. The trees blossom from spring to early summer and their fruits, or drupes (the pecans), look a bit like long walnuts and have a sweet taste.

Pistachio

It can take up to 10 years before this tree species is old enough to bear nuts. There are male and female pistachio trees. Both are needed to produce the delicious nuts. Pistachio trees prefer hot summers and cold winters. Pistachios are a popular snack to nibble on and there is also pistachio ice cream.

Walnut

Walnut trees bloom in late spring and are known not just for their nuts, but their wood too, which is often used in furniture-making. They thrive in temperate regions, growing in valleys and along rivers, and as high as 100 feet (30 meters)!

Trees and Us

Trees are a super-important part of our daily lives, not just because they produce oxygen. The wood we get from them can be used to build homes, make furniture, and create musical instruments. The paper we write on, many of the toys we play with, and even some boats start out as trees.

Many houses are built using wood from trees. One of the oldest wooden buildings in the world is the Hōryū-ji temple in Japan. It was originally built in the early 7th century, although after a fire it was reconstructed in the 8th century. It is a remarkable example of wooden architecture!

Wooden toys such as stacking blocks are popular with lots of children.

Books, like the one you are reading right now, are made from trees that are processed into paper then printed with words and pictures.

The beautiful sounds that instruments such as violins, guitars, and cellos make are possible thanks to the wood they're made from.

The paper you fold into fun shapes such as airplanes comes from trees.

The wood that crackles and pops in a campfire once stood as a tree in a forest.

The tissue paper you blow your nose on starts its journey to you as a tree.

The amber in your jewelry began as resin from trees that grew millions of years ago.

Many boats, such as canoes, are crafted from wood.

The maple syrup you drizzle on your pancakes starts as sap from the maple tree.

Trees and You

Trees and woodlands offer endless fun and adventure. You can climb trees, explore trails, and spot amazing wildlife such as woodpeckers, butterflies, squirrels, and maybe even slowworms or lizards! Woodlands are like a playground where you can rest, play, and discover new things every time you visit.

Ask an adult if they can build you a treehouse or put up a swing on a sturdy tree branch.

Read a book in the shade of a tree.

Have a picnic with a friend among the trees.

Take a little nap under a tree.

Climb trees with your friends—but always take care!

Take a gentle stroll through the woods.

DID YOU KNOW?

Woodland walks are a great way to enjoy nature and calm your mind. Also, in some places walkways have been built high up in the treetops!

True or False?

1. An oak tree is coniferous.

2. Maple trees produce sap that can be made into syrup.

3. Coniferous trees lose their leaves in winter.

4. Trees provide oxygen for us to breathe.

5. All trees have flowers.

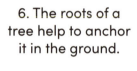

6. The roots of a tree help to anchor it in the ground.

7. Leaves from deciduous trees change color in the fall.

8. Palm trees are usually found in cold climates.

9. A tree's growth rings can tell us its age.

10. Some of the largest trees in the world are redwoods.

11. Giant sequoia trees are protected from the heat of forest fires by thick bark.

12. Birds build nests in trees for protection and raising their young.

1. FALSE / 2. TRUE / 3. FALSE / 4. TRUE / 5. FALSE / 6. TRUE / 7. TRUE / 8. FALSE / 9. TRUE / 10. TRUE / 11. TRUE / 12. TRUE

Let's Get Crafty!

Leaf prints

Collect a selection of leaves from outside, then paint them with a brush and your favorite colors. Press the painted leaves onto a piece of white paper or card to create a beautiful print. Their unique veins and shapes will create intricate patterns.

Pinecone bird feeder

Create a bird feeder by tying a piece of string to a pinecone, then make a spreadable paste from unsalted fat (beef or coconut fat) mixed with seeds, oats, and some flour and spread it all over the pinecone. Hang it on a branch and watch as birds enjoy a tasty treat!

Twig picture frames

Gather some clean, dry twigs from the ground, your favorite photo, and a piece of cardboard that is about 1 inch (3 centimeters) larger on all sides than your photo. Use white glue to attach the twigs around the edges of the cardboard. Once the glue is dry, place your photo in the center of the frame, securing it with sticky tack.